Prima Hernandia

Analysis and Implementation Genetic Algorithms on Random Early Detection

GRIN Publishing

Bibliographic information published by the German National Library:

The German National Library lists this publication in the National Bibliography; detailed bibliographic data are available on the Internet at http://dnb.dnb.de .

Imprint:

Copyright © 2012 GRIN Verlag GmbH
Print and binding: Books on Demand GmbH, Norderstedt Germany
ISBN: 978-3-656-92797-6

This book at GRIN:

http://www.grin.com/en/e-book/192774/analysis-and-implementation-genetic-algorithms-on-random-early-detection

GRIN - Your knowledge has value

Since its foundation in 1998, GRIN has specialized in publishing academic texts by students, college teachers and other academics as e-book and printed book. The website www.grin.com is an ideal platform for presenting term papers, final papers, scientific essays, dissertations and specialist books.

Visit us on the internet:

http://www.grin.com/

http://www.facebook.com/grincom

http://www.twitter.com/grin_com

Analysis and Implementation Genetic Algorithms on Random Early Detection

Prima Hernandia , Hendrawan

[1,2]Sekolah Tinggi Elektro dan Informatika, Institut Teknologi Bandung
Jl. Ganesha no. 10, Bandung, Indonesia

Abstraksi— **Application requirements for delay and low jitter has driven the development of Active Queue Management (AQM) is very fast. Random Early Detection (RED) as one of the AQM has grown so rapidly and become a reference for the development of other AQM variants. RED to be fast growing because of its simplicity and ease to modified its parameter. There have been many studies that discuss the development of RED, but very few have focused on finding w_q value, the weights for the optimal packet drop probability. In this study we tried to offer a different approach to the search w_q values using genetic algorithms. This is done to adapt the possible values w_q dynamically according to the character of traffic.**

Keywords— **RED, w_q value, dynamic traffic, genetic algorithms.**

I. INTRODUCTION

This Active queue management (AQM) has grown so rapidly by using a different approach. Generally aims to improve the performance of Transmission Control Protocol / Internet Protocol which has been recommended by the Internet Engineering Task Force (IETF) for the next generation router. In RFC 2309 [1] one of the goals is to maximize throughput AQM received by the user. The approach to AQM can be classified on the basis of the solution space search, as follows:

Table I-1 AQM Classification

Solution Space	AQM Method
Deterministic	ECN, Drop Tail
Heuristic	RED, ARED, SRED, FRED, RED-PD, CHOKe, BLUE
Optimization Theory	E-RED, REM
Control Theory	PI, PIP

Active Queue Management was first introduced by using the addition of bits of ECN as a mechanism of preventive control of the congestion. These control bits are not doing any calculations, but only as a status that is marked on the package to be dropped when congestion occurs. The use of ECN bits first introduced by the Network Working Group RFC in the recommendations. Currently what happens is congestion on

the network transport layer was detected on. In the paper [2], the author gives a suggestion that congestion should be detected before a buffer overflow and packet should be dropped. ECN RFC proposes the addition of two bits in IP header to indicate the occurrence of congestion. Proposed solution with addition of ECN bits can not be directly implemented, at least there are some considerations, there are Routers that do not support the ECN mechanism must have the ability to support migration to ECN, congestion control mechanisms that exist should still be used. In the RFC states that reserved addition of 2 bits (6 and 7) is used to indicates status of the packet flow. The use of these bits is as follows:

Table I-2 ECN Bit Indicator

Bit Indicator	Keterangan
00	Packet does not use ECN
10 atau 01	Packet use ECN, but there is no congestion.
11	Packet using ECN, but there is no congestion.

If the received packet with ECN code 11 and packet will be dropped, then the congestion window to be halved. Mechanisms used to avoid data loss during transmission by providing prior notification before congestion occurs.

Different approach was done by using Drop Tail as described in [3]. Authors in [3] provides a simple solution to deal with congestion on the router. We used to know that Drop Tail is naive handling of overflow traffic. If the packet is coming and it will be queued unserved prior in long queues with static queue, the queue when it comes unhandled again so the next packet will be dropped. It is occur when the arrival time is much faster than the router service time.

FIFO approach such as the Drop Tail buffer overflow condition is very prone to global synchronization, which dropped packets from different connections. Conditions of global synchronization, causing the window size decreases and the impact on the overall throughput. This is a concern in the paper [3] with the development of mechanisms of Random Early Detection (RED) to avoid congestion. The main focus of the development of this mechanism is to maintain long average queue in the router keep it short. This is made possible by a specific packet drop or mark placed in the queue exceeds certain limits. Queuing system by using RED queue defining Q_{min} and Q_{max} as upper and lower limits. At the time the package arrived, this system will calculate Q_{avg} of the incoming flow and compared with Q_{min} and Q_{max}. Q_{avg} values updated every new package comes with the formula: $Q_{avg} = (1 - W_q) \times Q_{avg} + W_q \times Q_{curr}$, where the value W_q is weight of the average queue length before and Q_{curr} is a current queue length at this time.

If Q_{avg} exceed Q_{max} then the packet is marked, whereas if the value Q_{avg} is between Q_{min} and Q_{max} then the probability of packet marker P_m can be searched with the following formula: $P_m = \frac{P_{avg}}{1-count.P_{avg}}$ where the value of count is the number of packets since last packet is marked. P_{avg} defined as follows: $P_{avg} = P_m^{max} \times \frac{Q_{avg}-Q_{min}}{Q_{max}-Q_{min}}$. Packet characterized by the probability P_m, in this case the count is reset. If the package is not marked, then the count will increase. This mechanism allows the average queue length can be controlled and avoid congestion.

RED still has limitations with parameters that are static. Floyd, Gummadi, and Shenker in the paper [4] did a little modification to the RED. Adaptive-RED mechanism capable of adapting to changes in parameters of RED based on the existing situation. The parameters used in the RED Adapative similar to those used previously. RED randomly discarding packets with a probability according to the average queue length. Only congestion and parameter setting has an effect on the balance between link utilization and delay the rendah.ARED as described in [4], the parameter adaptation to reduce the packet loss rate and variance of queue length.

In the previous RED development is emphasized to regulate the average queue length so that variance is not too volatile, fairness issues remain unresolved as well. In the paper [5] The issue was raised, Stabilized RED (SRED) is developed by taking into account the current flow. The number of active flows recorded (zombie list), each zombie list can consist of more than one entry per flow. Counter value of independent, not dependent on any list though zombies represent the same flow. If the new package and then the zombie corresponding counter value increases, if the opposite occurs according to the probability of the identifier of the zombie P_{over} rewritten with the identification of a new package and the counter value at reset.

Managing of different traffic flow is also become main focus in paper [6], constraints on the RED which is not fair sharing of bandwidth in different traffic. RED does not consider to bandwidth utilization of related current flow will do drop packets. FRED on paper [6] proposed to utilize the bandwidth per flow to reduce the loss of each flow, resulting in overall bandwidth utilization. The main purpose of FRED is to provide a different strategy to drop packets of different flows. The new parameters used in the model queue. Q^{min} and Q^{max} represent the number of packets of flow i is accommodated in the buffer. Q_{avg}^{min} and Q_{avg}^{max} is the maximum

and minimum size of an average size of the buffer. Q_i is the current number of packets in flow i and Q_{avg} is the average size of the buffer in the system.

If the paper [6] handling of packet drop done by looking at the behavior of current flow and does not depend on previous conditions, different approaches conducted in paper [7] through the RED-Preferential Dropping (RED-PD), the mechanism is to use the previous and dropping notes identify a flow that uses a large bandwidth. When the detected on the record, dropped packets have a relationship with a certain flow over the next packet is chosen to be dropped. RED-PD is only active when there is not enough bandwidth is sufficient for all the flow and do drop certain packets to be normal bandwidth.

At the time of arrival of packets, detect whether the system violates the bandwidth limitation, in the event that the packet will be dropped based on the specific flow characteristics. If no violation is detected, then the probability limit bandwidth drop to comply with the usual RED.

RED Development by observing to flow conditions was conducted in a choke mechanism [8]. Choke mechanism using the same parameters with the RED and the only active if there is congestion $(Q_{avg} > Q_{min})$. The main idea of this mechanism is a new package comes as compared m random packet in the queue. Each package is identified originating from the same flow will be dropped. If not from the same flow the choke will do a maximum utilization of the queue if $(Q_{avg} > Q_{max})$. If there is maximum utilization of the new packet will be dropped. When utilization is not maximized then the packet is queued with probability P equal to the probability of the RED drop. Parameter m is the number of packets that will be compared with the new package. Mechanism more effective use of bandwidth than RED in high-speed transmission.

Lia et al. developed with Exponential RED RED (E-RED) as in paper [9]. This mechanism uses the primal-dual solution as used in the optimization theory to calculate the parameters for the RED drop. Parameters used in the E-RED is Q_{min} and Q_{max} as queue length threshold, Q_{avg} is the average queue length, C is a capacity of the system, Q_c is the current queue length, P_m^{min} is the minimum probability of packet drop at $Q_c > Q_{min}$. Packet drop probability value is calculated with the following conditions:

$$P_m = \begin{cases} 0 & if\ 0 \leq Q_C \leq Q_{min} \\ P_m^{min} \times e^{\frac{Q_c \times (Q_c - Q_{min})}{c}} & if\ Q_{min} \leq Q_C \leq Q_{max} \\ 1 & if\ Q_{max} \leq Q_C \end{cases}$$

Pengembangan RED dengan memperhatikan kondisi flow juga dilakukan dalam mekanisme CHOKe [8]. Mekanisme CHOKe menggunakan parameter yang sama dengan RED dan hanya aktif bila terjadi kongesti $(Q_{avg} > Q_{min})$. Ide utama dari mekanisme ini adalah paket yang baru datang dibandingkan m paket secara random dalam antrian. Setiap paket yang teridentifikasi berasal dari flow yang sama akan didrop. Apabila tidak berasal dari flow yang sama maka CHOKe akan melakukan pemeriksaan apakah utilisasi maksimal antrian $(Q_{avg} > Q_{max})$. Jika terjadi utilisasi maksimal maka paket baru akan didrop. Bila utilisasi belum maksimal maka paket akan diantrikan dengan probabilitas P yang besarnya sama dengan probabilitas drop pada RED. Parameter m adalah jumlah paket yang akan dibandingkan dengan paket baru. Mekanisme menggunakan bandwidth lebih efektif dibandingkan RED dalam transmisi kecepatan tinggi.

Lia *et al.* mengembangkan RED dengan Exponential RED (E-RED) seperti dalam paper [9]. Mekanisme ini menggunakan solusi primal-dual seperti yang digunakan dalam teori optimasi untuk menghitung parameter drop untuk RED. Parameter yang digunakan dalam E-RED yaitu Q_{min} dan Q_{max} sebagai ambang batas panjang antrian, Q_{avg} adalah panjang antrian rata-rata, C adalah besar kapasitas dari system, Q_c adalah panjang antrian saat ini, P_m^{min} adalah probabilitas minimum drop paket pada saat $Q_c > Q_{min}$. Nilai probabilitas drop paket dihitung dengan ketentuan sebagai berikut :

$$P_m = \begin{cases} 0 & if \ 0 \leq Q_C \leq Q_{min} \\ P_m^{min} \times e^{\frac{Q_c \times (Q_c - Q_{min})}{c}} & if \ Q_{min} \leq Q_C \leq Q_{max} \\ 1 & if \ Q_{max} \leq Q_C \end{cases}$$

Unlike the previous methods that emphasize handling flow, and Srikant Kunniyur the paper [10] observe the stability of the queue length of Adaptive Virtual Queue mechanism Algorithm (AVQ). AVQ keep the queue length remains low to reduce the delay end-to-end user experience. AVQ using a virtual queue with a capacity smaller than the real queue. At the time of arrival of the virtual queue length will increase and if full then packets dropped. At the time the packet leaves the virtual queue, the virtual queue length will be reduced. AVQ does not require the probability of droping the package and set the link utilization by providing feedback to flow sources. Unlike to the RED, the queue length fluctuations of low and stable.

Unlike the previous approach that is more deterministic, Hollot et. al. on paper [11] using theory of control that is able to develop the RED queue length set and maintain the queuing delay remains small. This approach uses the current queue length as feedback for the current link utilization and designing control Proportional Integral (PI) as appropriate. Simply drop in the probability of packet marker interval of time t can be calculated as follows:

$$P_t = a \times \Delta Q(t) - b \times \Delta Q(t-1) + P(t-1)$$

Where is $\Delta Q(t) = Q_{curr}(t) - Q_{target}$, Q_{target} is a target queue length, a and b are coefficients. If the queue length close to the target queue length can be said system in steady-state conditions.

The principle used in [11] developed by Heying et. al. in the paper [12] through a Proportional Integral Controller with Position Feedback Compensation (PIP). PIP was developed to improve the robustness and speed of response of the system. In this system the probability of packet drop marker depends not only on the current queue length and queue length but also the tendency of the target queue length. PIP PI in terms of improving the accuracy and sensitivity of parameter changes.

In the previous discussion of RED development and performance measurement of congestion are not separated, but become a unity. Different approaches do Athuraliya et al. in the paper [13] to deal with congestion problems. In the method of Random Exponential Marking (REM), they separate the congestion and performance measurement. Measurements include the need for bandwidth congestion and the number of active users, while keeping the focus on performance measurement packet loss and delay remains small. Performance is measured in the queue length and loss, while congestion is measured in price, the weight of the arrival rate and queue, the value is changed periodically.

BLUE algorithm developed by Feng et al. in the paper [14] see idle time factor as an opportunity to reduce congestion. BLUE uses packet loss and link idle time on the output as an indicator of congestion and the need to be addressed to prevent loss and reduce the rate of oscillation of the length of the queue. The main idea is to increase the probability of packet drop markers on arrival in δ_1 time intervals and the probability decreases as the idle condition, δ_2 if the length of time between δ_1 and δ_2 greater than the freeze-time. δ_1 value must be greater than δ_2.

II. BACKGROUND

Random Early Detection (RED) as one of the AQM itself occupies a very large portion of the development because of its easy implementation by exploring four main parameters of the queue. Problems in RED are basically focused on throughput, fairness, delay and jitter which is the main problem Active Queue Management (AQM). Several methods have been developed based on the conditions and the focus of each issue as it has been discussed previously.

Based on the description of the development of RED has been discussed previously, the main parameters of the four most commonly used on the parameter setting is Q_{min}, Q_{max}, and P_m^{max} according with the quality of the connection parameters and types of traffic (TCP and UDP) without regard to the optimal value w_q . W_q value must be carefully selected short-term increase in long queues during congestion in congested conditions did not significantly affect the average queue length. On the other hand, the increase in value w_q in the long term will lead to more persistent congestion and ultimately affect the average queue length.

W_q values affect the sensitivity of the average queue length as a function of queue length sesaaat. W_q values that are too small will cause the average queue length is too slow to react to the increase in long-term queue digateway. If the value is too large w_q will impact the average queue length is changing too quickly and fail to filter out transient congestion at the queue. As a parameter that is used to obtain the average queue length, it is important to choose the right w_q.

RED itself has no single solution to resolve the congestion conditions, no single set of parameters that can be applicable to all conditions. RED has the solution space to obtain the four main parameters are very broad and the search should be carried out heuristic.

III. GENETIC ALGORITHMS

Genetic Algorithm (GA) is an algorithm inspired by evolutionary theory of Charles Darwin. Search for a solution of the problem is done by a gradual process of evolution. Suyanto in [20] states that the genetic algorithm gives the solution of problems which do not have a definitive solution search method.

1. Initial Population

Population is a collection of some individuals. All populations in the genetic algorithm is derived from a population that is the initial population. Solution or the best chromosome of the initial population will be maintained, and will have the possibility of an evolutionary process to get a better solution.

Preparation of the initial population is done through a process of random selection from all the existing solutions. This random selection led to the initial population of genetic algorithms will not be the same in each experiment, although the same parameters used. Population is a chromosome that represents the value of EWMA weight estimator (w_q), in a binary number.

2. Fitness Function

To find out whether or not the solutions that exist on an individual, each individual in the population must have a value for comparison (fitness cost). The best solution would be retained, while other solutions be changed to obtain another solution, through the stages of crossover and mutation (mutation). Fitness function is the thing that distinguishes genetic algorithm implementation in different cases.

Evaluation performed on best value by the method of Mean Squared Error (MSE) on a subset of data from the entire data length of the queue for a moment. Any individual who raised a representation of the value of a queue weight (w_q) will be tested fitness through EWMA estimator function to get the new instantaneous value of the queue.

3. Selection

MSE value has been obtained for each weight EWMA (w_q) will be added in stages from the first MSE value is generated. Each MSE value will be the proportion of the total value generated by the specific weight (w_q). The value of this proportion to be compared with the probability of a random selection using a roulette wheel mechanisms.

4. Cross Over

Crossover process will cross two of the best individuals in a population, to get two new individuals. After the selection phase, it will obtain a new population of 2-times amount of the old population.

5. Mutation

Another process to get two new individuals by mutation. The probability of occurrence of mutations in the gene on a chromosome is very small, because in its application to genetic algorithm, the probability is often made of small,

smaller than 0.5 (mutation rate). Unlike the crossover phase, in which one individual need to cross with another individual, mutation phase does not require another individual to mutate.

Heuristic search techniques in the solution can be approximated by the method of Genetic Algorithm. In view of the solution space for the parameter values included in the class of NP-hard, meaning there is no definite solution of a calculation. Genetic algorithm is a heuristic approach that takes the principles of natural evolution through the selection phase, crossover, and mutation. In this paper tested a new technique to find the limit w_q by using a genetic algorithm.

IV. RED MODEL WITH GENETIC ALGORITHMS

In this study we propose a new approach to the problem of searching w_q values by using genetic algorithms. GaRED model developed based on the model RED and Simple Genetic Algorithms.

Figure IV-1 GaRED flow diagram

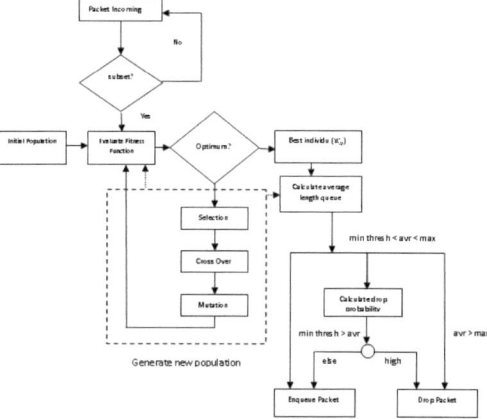

Each packet arrival and queue the incoming packet will be stored in a buffer which serves as a data sample collector. If the amount has reached a specified subset at the beginning, the system is determined 200 samples, then conducted the evaluation process. Meanwhile, on the other system, the algorithm GA generate random number of populations, the system is determined five individuals, then the input to the evaluation process. Together with the data buffer, the system will evaluate all input. Each individual is raised will result in a certain MSE value was calculated as follows

$$MSE = \frac{\sum_{i=0}^{n-1}(avg - avg_{thres})^2}{n}$$

Where n is the number of sampling, avg is the average steady-state queue length, avg_{thres} average queue is obtained by calculating reference

$$avg_{thres} = \frac{min_{th} + max_{th}}{2}$$

Individuals who produce a minimum MSE will be the new population. This population will undergo a selection process by the method of the roulette wheel, one point crossover, and mutation of the event. Best individual (   ) will be an input to calculate steady-state average queue length of RED.

V. RESULT AND ANALYSIS

Performance testing conducted by observing at the throughput generated during the observation period. Simulation using a simple topology to minimize the influence of factors other than the parameters to be tested.

Figure V-1 Simulation Diagram

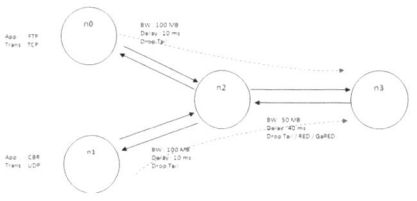

Terdapat parameter yang akan diuji pengaruhnya terhadap performa yaitu : rata-rata panjang paket, rata-rata waktu antar kedatangan, dan panjang antrian.

There are parameters to be tested its effect on performance : the average packet length, the average inter-arrival time, and queue length.

1. Average packet length effect

The average length of the packet according Crovella [19] distributed pareto. In the experiment will be assumed value of fixed shape, which is 1.2 and the average value of [2500 .. 20 000]. Obtained the following result

Table V-1 Average packet length effect

Average packet length (Byte)	Throughput (MBps)		
	DT	RED	GaRED
2500	336	233	630
5000	531	468	1009
7500	729	838	1865
10000	1041	799	2652
15000	2642	1440	2110
20000	1133	2375	2440

In the table above shows that the throughput produced by GaRED have a tendency to increase and have huge differences in the average packet length less than 10 KB. Meanwhile, the average length of more than 10 KB packet

Figure V-2 Throughput tren vs packet length

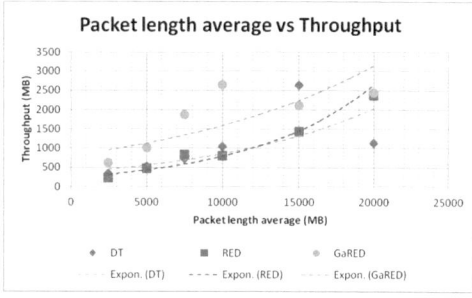

throughput resulting difference gets smaller when compared with RED. Throughput growth trend can be seen as follows:

2. Average inter-arrival time effect

Inter-arrival time for traffic with small-scale connections can be modeled with a Poisson distribution as stated in Crovella [19]. Inter-arrival time distribution is influenced by the arrival rate λ, where the average inter-arrival time is $1 / \lambda$. Average value to be used is $[0.05 .. 0.5]$. Obtained the following results:

Table V-2 Inter-arrival time effect

Inter-arrival time (ms)	Throughput (MBps)		
	DT	RED	GaRED
0,05	2266	749	1219
0,1	842	478	830
0,15	452	472	504
0,2	463	524	2430
0,25	494	536	715
0,3	448	497	506
0,35	416	609	772
0,4	451	501	1928
0,45	631	723	610
0,5	823	647	637

In the above table can be seen that when the average inter-packet arrival time 0.2 ms and 0.4 ms, produced GaRED throughput reaches the maximum value. Meanwhile, the average inter-packet arrival time of 0.05 ms GaRED throughput is better than Drop Tail. Throughput growth trend can be seen in the picture below

Figure V-3 Throughput tren vs inter-arrival time

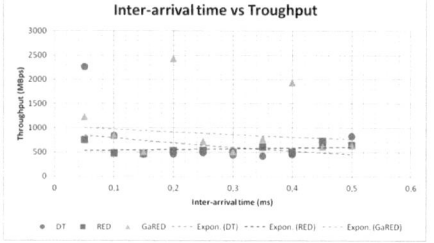

3. Queue length effect

Scenario is performed to see the influence of the queue length of produced throughput by using Drop Tail queue management, RED, and GaRED. In this scenario used the average packet length of 10 KB and the average time between the arrival of 0.2 ms. Observations shown in the table below :

Table V-3 Queue length effect

Queue Length (Byte)	Throughput (MBps)		
	DT	RED	GaRED
200	51108	49578	23754
400	43898	84142	34658
600	42739	92520	45971
800	48547	49070	65003
1000	86593	30441	158862
1500	26572	30381	74946
2000	166960	40061	148545

Based on the above experimental results, it appears that the use of queue management GaRED will reach the maximum value specified when the queue length of 1000 bytes. In the queue length of 200 Byte performance is better than GaRED DropTail and RED. This happens because at the time of the queue length is not large, then the data packet will be faster to fill the queue. Data packets that can not be enqueued will be dropped because it will be for the packet-marking process itself, which takes more time than discard the packet directly. Meanwhile, the growth trend of higher throughput

Figure V-4 Tren throughput vs queue length

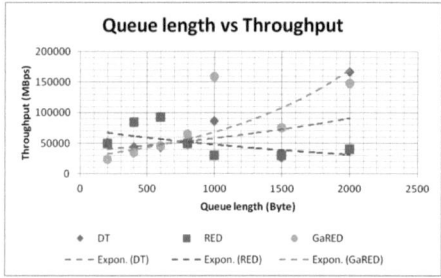

VI. CONCLUSION

Genetic Algorithm implementation has been done on the Random Early Detection, produces some of the conclusions are :

(1) Implementation of Genetic Algorithm can be done on the Random Early Detection by observing computational constraints of the GA as it affects the delay that arise in the node.

(2) Effect of the average length of the packet throughput appears on the package with a length less than 10 KB. In the packet length is above the 10 MB it is clear that

the performance improvement compared to Drop Tail GaRED and RED is not very significant.

(3) Effect of inter-arrival time of the average of the throughput seen at the time of arrival is determined between 0.2 to 0.4 ms. At that range GaRED performance results show its maximum throughput, whereas in the range below 0.2 ms even better performance than RED, but still not better than Drop Tail.

(4) Effect of length queue to throughput be seen as length queue increases. Under conditions where the queue length over 800 bytes, the throughput produced by GaRED increased significantly.

REFERENCE

[1] Braden B, Clark D, Crowcroft J, Davie B, Deering S, Estrin D, Floyd S, Jacobson V, Minshall G, Partridge C,Peterson L, Ramakrishnan K, Shenker S, Wroclawski J, Zhang L. Recommendations on queue management and congestion avoidance in the Internet. *RFC 2309*, April 1998.

[2] K. Ramakrishnan, S. Floyd, and D. Black. RFC 3168, The Addition of Explicit Congestion Notification (ECN) to IP. 2001.

[3] Sally Floyd and Van Jacobson. Random early detection gateways for congestion avoidance. *IEEE/ACM Trans. Netw.*, 1(4):397–413, 1993.

[4] Sally Floyd, Ramakrishna Gummadi, , and Scott Shenker. Adaptive red : An algorithm for increasing the robustness of red's active queue management. Technical report, 2001.

[5] Teunis J. Ott, T. V. Lakshman, and Larry H. Wong. SRED: Stabilized RED. In *Proceedings of INFOCOM*, volume 3, pages 1346–1355, 1999.

[6] Dong Lin and Robert Morris. Dynamics of random early detection. In *SIGCOMM '97: Proceedings of the ACM SIGCOMM '97 conference on Applications, technologies, architectures, and protocols for computer communication*, pages 127–137, New York, NY, USA, 1997. ACM Press.

[7] R. Mahajan, S. Floyd, and D. Wetherall. Controlling high-bandwidth flows at the congested router, 2001.

[8] Rong Pan, B. Prabhakar, and K. Psounis. CHOKe - a stateless active queue management scheme for approximating fair bandwidth allocation. 2:942–951, 2000.

[9] Shao Liu, Tamer Basar, and R. Srikant. Exponential-red: a stabilizing aqm scheme for low- and high-speed TCP protocols. *IEEE/ACM Trans. Netw.*,13(5):1068–1081, 2005.

[10] Srisankar S. Kunniyur and R. Srikant. An adaptive virtual

queue (avq) algorithm for active queue management. *IEEE/ACM Trans. Netw.*, 12(2) : 286–299, 2004.

[11] C. V. Hollot, V. Misra, D. Towsley, and W. Gong. On designing improved controllers for aqm routers supporting tcp flows. Technical report, Amherst,MA, USA, 2000.

[12] Zhang Heying, Liu Baohong, and Dou Wenhua. Design of a robust active queue management algorithm based on feedback compensation. In *SIGCOMM' 03: Proceedings of the 2003 conference on Applications, technologies, architectures, and protocols for computer communications*, pages 277–285, New York, NY, USA, 2003. ACM Press.

[13] Sanjeewa Athuraliya, Victor H. Li, Steven H. Low, and Qinghe Yin. REM: Active queue management. *IEEE Network*, 15(3):48 – 53, May/June 2001.

[14] Wu chang Feng, Kang G. Shin, Dilip D. Kandlur, and Debanjan Saha. The blue active queue management algorithms. *IEEE/ACM Trans. Netw.*, 10(4):513–528, 2002.

[15] Zheng. B, Atiquzzaman. M. A framework to determine the optimal weight parameter of RED in next-generation Internet routers. *International Journal of Communication System* **21**: 987–1008, 2008;

[16] V. Jacobson, K. Nichols, K. Poduri, "RED in a different Light", *Draft Technical Report*, Cisco Systems, Sept. 1999

[17] D. Veitch, J. Andren, M. Hilding, "Understanding end to end Internet traffic dynamics", *IEEE Globecom'98*, Melbourne, AU, 1998.

[18] Bonald. T, May. M, Bolot. J, "Analytic Evaluation of RED Performance", *IEEE INFOCOM 2000*, pp.1415-144.

[19] Crovella. M, Bestravos, "Self-similiarity in World Wide Web traffic: Evidence and possible cause", *ACM Sigmetrics*, 1996

[20] Suyanto, "Algoritma Genetika dalam MATLAB", *Penerbit Andi*, 2005